Nature Vs. Nurture: The Tale of Discrete Trial Training and Natural Environment Teaching

Travis Breeding

ISBN: 9798376526187

DEDICATION

THIS BOOK IS DEDICATED TO THE
MANY IDIVIDUALS IN THE WORLD
LIVING WITH ASD AND PEOPLE WHO
LOVE AND SUPPORT THEM. I HOPE
YOU FIND THIS BOOK USEFUL AND
HELPFUL ON YOUR JOURNEY

CONTENTS

ACKNOWLEDGMENTS

I'd to thank my friends and family for always being here
for me and allowing me the time to write. I appreciate all
you do for me.

1 INTRODUCTION TO NATURE VS NURTURE DEBATE IN ABA

Introduction to Discrete Trial Training and Natural Environment Teaching in Applied Behavior Analysis

Applied behavior analysis (ABA) is an evidence-based, scientifically validated approach to understanding and changing human behavior. It is used in a variety of settings, from classrooms and therapy centers to homes and hospitals. ABA is used to increase desirable behaviors,

decrease undesirable behaviors, and teach
new skills.

Discrete trial training (DTT) and natural
environment teaching (NET) are two
approaches to ABA. Both approaches are
evidence-based and have a strong
research foundation behind them, but the
methods and interventions used in each
approach are significantly different.

What is Discrete Trial Training?

Discrete trial training is a procedure-
based intervention in which learners are
taught new skills through a series of trial-
and-error drills. The drills are typically
presented one at a time, in a structured
and controlled environment. The learner
is presented with a task and provided

with a prompt, instruction, and reinforcement.

For example, if a teacher is teaching a student to recognize the letter "A", the student may first be presented with a series of pictures of objects that begin with the letter "A" (e.g., apple, ant, airplane). The teacher may prompt the student to identify each item by saying "what's this?" or "what letter does this start with?". If the student correctly identifies the letter, the teacher may provide positive reinforcement (e.g., verbal praise, a sticker, a token).

The purpose of DTT is to teach a learner specific skills that are broken down into small, achievable steps. It is a highly structured approach, and it requires a significant amount of time and resources to implement.

What is Natural Environment Teaching?

Natural environment teaching (NET) is a behavior-based approach in which learners are taught in natural settings. In NET, teachers use prompts to cue the learner to engage in a desired behavior—without the use of a drill or series of trials.

For example, if a teacher is teaching a student to recognize the letter "A", the student may be presented with a book that contains pictures of items that begin with the letter "A". The teacher may prompt the student to identify each item by pointing to the picture of the item and saying "what's this?" or "what letter does this start with?". If the student correctly identifies the letter, the teacher may provide positive reinforcement (e.g., verbal praise, a sticker, a token).

The purpose of NET is to teach a learner to respond to cues in a variety of settings and to generalize the skills they learn in one setting to other settings. It requires less time and resources to implement than DTT, and it promotes social interaction and independence.

Comparing Discrete Trial Training to Natural Environment Teaching

Discrete trial training and natural environment teaching are two distinct approaches to ABA. While both approaches are evidence-based and have a strong research foundation behind them, the methods and interventions used in each approach are significantly different.

DTT is a procedure-based intervention in which learners are taught new skills through a series of trial-and-error drills. DTT is a highly structured approach, and it requires a significant amount of time and resources to implement.

NET is a behavior-based approach in which learners are taught in natural settings. NET requires less time and resources to implement than DTT, and it promotes social interaction and independence.

When deciding which approach to use, it

is important to consider the learner's individual needs, the resources available, and the type of skills that need to be taught. Depending on the learner, one approach may be more effective than the other. It is also important to recognize that both approaches have a place in ABA, and that they can be used in combination to provide a comprehensive program of instruction.

2 A HISTORICAL OVERVIEW OF DISCRETE TRIAL TRAINING

Discrete trial training (DTT) is an effective method of applied behavior analysis (ABA) used to teach important skills to children with autism. It is an evidence-based practice that has been successfully used to teach children with autism to acquire academic, social, communication, and adaptive living skills. The use of discrete trial training in ABA has proven to be a successful method for teaching children with autism.

Discrete trial training (DTT) is a teaching

technique derived from ABA. It is based on the premise that behavior can be analyzed, observed, and changed. DTT is used to systematically teach children with autism to acquire a wide range of skills. During a discrete trial session, an instructor presents a child with an opportunity to respond to a stimulus. The child is then rewarded for correctly responding to the stimulus with praise or a tangible reward. The reward reinforces the desired behavior, thereby increasing the likelihood that the behavior will occur again in the future.

In a typical discrete trial session, the instructor presents a child with a stimulus. For example, the instructor may present a child with a toy animal and ask, "What is this?" The instructor will then wait for the child to make a response. If the child responds correctly, the instructor will provide praise or a tangible reward to reinforce the correct response. If the child responds incorrectly, the instructor will provide a prompt, such as pointing to the animal and saying, "This is a dog." The instructor will then wait for the child to make a response again. If the child responds correctly, the instructor will provide praise or a tangible reward.

Discrete trial training is a powerful tool used to teach children with autism a variety of skills. It has been successfully used to teach children with autism to acquire academic skills, such as recognizing numbers or letters, counting, and reading simple words. DTT has also been used to teach children with autism to acquire social skills, such as following directions, taking turns, initiating interaction with peers, and understanding personal space. In addition, discrete trial training has been used to teach children with autism to acquire communication skills, such as understanding language, using words to communicate, and expressing emotions. Finally, discrete trial training has been used to teach children with autism to acquire adaptive living skills, such as dressing themselves, brushing their teeth, and eating with utensils.

When implementing discrete trial training, it is important to use a systematic teaching approach. It is also important to ensure that the instruction is tailored to a child's individual needs and abilities. For example, if a child is able to understand and respond to verbal stimuli, then verbal instruction should be used. However, if a child is not able to understand or respond to verbal stimuli, then visual prompts should be used. Additionally, the instructor should adjust the difficulty level of the instruction to ensure that the child is able to accurately respond to the stimulus.

In order to ensure the effectiveness of discrete trial training, it is important to end each session with a reinforcer. A reinforcer is a reward that reinforces the desired behavior and increases the likelihood that the behavior will occur again in the future. The most commonly used reinforcer in DTT is praise. Praise is an effective reinforcer because it is immediate and does not require a tangible reward. Additionally, the instructor can provide additional reinforcing activities, such as allowing the child to play with a toy, watch a video, or engage in a preferred activity.

Discrete trial training is an effective method of teaching skills to children with autism. It is based on the principle that behavior can be analyzed, observed, and changed. During a discrete trial session, an instructor presents a child with a stimulus and rewards the child for correctly responding to the stimulus with praise or a tangible reward. Discrete trial training has been successfully used to teach children with autism to acquire a wide range of skills, including academic, social, communication, and adaptive living skills. In order to ensure the effectiveness of discrete trial training, it is important to use a systematic teaching approach and to end each session with a reinforcer.

3 NATURAL ENVIRONMENT TEACHING: ORIGINS AND EVOLUTION

Natural environment teaching (NET) is a type of instruction that engages learners in activities and instruction that take place in the natural environment. This type of learning focuses on teaching through real-life activities, rather than through traditional methods such as lectures and worksheets. Natural environment teaching is often used to teach social skills and other necessary life skills to individuals with disabilities. It can also be used to help children learn to explore their environment and develop better communication skills. It is an effective way to provide specialized instruction in an individualized and meaningful way.

Natural environment teaching involves taking the learning environment out of the traditional classroom setting and into a natural setting, such as a park, a playground, or even a backyard. This allows students to interact with their environment and each other in a natural way. The teacher is present in the environment, but is not necessarily "teaching" in the typical sense of the word. The teacher is there to facilitate learning and to observe the interactions of the students.

One example of a natural environment teaching activity is the use of role-play. Role-play is an activity in which the students act out a particular scenario, such as a conversation between two people or a group of people. The teacher is present to provide feedback and guidance, but it is the students that are doing the talking and interacting. This activity allows the students to practice their social skills in a natural setting and to get comfortable with recognizing and responding to different social cues.

Other examples of natural environment teaching activities include exploring the environment, such as a park or garden, practicing communication skills in a small-group setting, or using the outdoors to practice gross motor skills such as running and jumping. These activities can be tailored to the individual's needs and interests, as well as their current level of ability.

Natural environment teaching has several benefits for learners. First, it provides an opportunity for students to practice their skills in a natural setting, which can help them generalize their skills to other contexts. For example, if a student is practicing communicating effectively in a small group setting in the park, this skill can be applied to other small group settings, such as in the classroom.

Second, natural environment teaching allows learners to interact with their environment in a meaningful way. By exploring their environment, learners can develop a better understanding of how the world works and how they can interact with it. This can be especially beneficial for learners who are learning to communicate or interact with others, as it can help them understand the reactions of those around them.

Finally, natural environment teaching provides an opportunity for learners to engage with their peers in meaningful ways. By interacting with their peers in a natural setting, learners can practice their social skills and gain a better understanding of how to interact and communicate. This can help learners develop better relationships with their peers and learn to interact more effectively in different contexts.

Overall, natural environment teaching is an effective way to provide specialized instruction in an individualized and meaningful way. By providing learners with the opportunity to interact with their environment and each other in a natural setting, natural environment teaching allows learners to generalize and apply their skills to different contexts. This can help learners develop better communication and social skills and gain a better understanding of how the world works. Natural environment teaching is a great way to foster meaningful learning and help learners grow and develop.

4 SOCIAL VALIDITY IN ABA

Applied behavior analysis (ABA) is a

scientifically-based approach to understanding human behavior and helping people learn more effective ways of interacting with the environment. Within ABA, there is a concept called "social validity" which is the extent to which an intervention is accepted, valued, and supported by those directly and indirectly involved in the intervention. The concept of social validity is important to ABA practitioners because interventions that are accepted and supported by all parties involved (e.g. the individual receiving the intervention, the family, and the professionals providing the intervention) are more likely to be successful and be maintained over time.

In ABA, natural environment teaching (NET) has been found to have higher social validity than discrete trial training (DTT). Natural environment teaching is a technique in which the individual is taught in their natural environment and is taught skills that are relevant to the environment where the teaching takes place. Additionally, NET does not require the individual to be in a structured environment, such as a classroom, or to follow a strict teaching schedule. Instead, NET allows the individual to learn skills in their natural environment, at their own pace, and in a more naturalistic way.

Discrete trial training, on the other hand, requires the individual to be in a more structured environment and to follow a predictable schedule of teaching activities and responses. Additionally, the skills that are taught in DTT may not be relevant to the individual's natural environment, which can make it more difficult for the individual to generalize the learned skills to different environments. This can be especially problematic if the individual is expected to use the skills they have acquired in DTT in various real-world settings.

For these reasons, NET has been found to have higher social validity than DTT. The acceptance and support of those involved in NET is often higher as the individual is able to learn in their natural environment, at their own pace, and with skills that are relevant to the environment. In contrast, DTT can often be seen as a more rigid and structured approach to teaching, which can lead to lower levels of acceptance and support from those involved.

In addition to having higher social validity, NET also has the advantage of allowing the individual to learn skills that are relevant to the environment in which they will be using the skills. This is important as it allows the individual to more easily generalize the learned skills to different environments. In contrast, DTT may not teach skills that are relevant to the environment in which the individual will be using the skills, making it more difficult for them to apply the learned skills to different environments.

For these reasons, it is important for ABA practitioners to consider incorporating natural environment teaching into their treatment plans. Below are five tips for how to apply NET to a learner's treatment plan that can help the learner generalize and apply skills in different environments.

1. Identify the environment where the individual will be using the learned skills. This is important as it allows the ABA practitioner to determine which skills are most relevant to the environment and can be taught through NET.

2. Identify the individual's current skills and what skills they need to learn in order to be successful. This is important as it allows the ABA practitioner to determine which skills can be taught through NET and what skills need to be taught through a more structured approach.

3. Develop a plan for teaching the individual the skills that are relevant to the environment in which they will be using the skills. This plan should include

activities that are specific to the
individual's needs, as well as activities
that are designed to help the individual
generalize the learned skills to different
environments.

4. Provide frequent and immediate
feedback to the individual about their
performance. This will help the
individual to understand their progress
and will encourage them to continue
using the skills in different environments.

5. Monitor the individual's progress and
adjust the plan, as needed. This is
important as it allows the ABA
practitioner to ensure that the individual
is learning the skills and is able to
generalize the skills to different
environments.

In conclusion, social validity is an important concept in ABA and natural environment teaching has been found to have higher levels of social validity than discrete trial training. Additionally, NET has the advantage of allowing the individual to learn skills that are more relevant to the environment in which they will be using the skills, which can help to increase the likelihood that the individual will be able to generalize and apply the skills in different environments. By following the five tips outlined above, ABA practitioners can incorporate NET into their treatment plans, helping the individual to increase their levels of success and generalize the skills they have learned.

5 DEFINING AUTISM

Introduction

Autism is a developmental disorder that affects an individual's ability to interact and communicate with others. People with autism often struggle to understand the nuances of social interactions, and they can find it difficult to understand the concept of generalizing and applying social skills to different social situations.

This can have a profound impact on their life, as it can make it difficult for them to form meaningful relationships with others. Fortunately, with the help of a qualified professional, such as a Board Certified Behavior Analyst (BCBA), autistic individuals can learn effective strategies to generalize and apply social skills across different social environments. The purpose of this essay is to explore the role of a BCBA in helping to teach autistic individuals how to generalize and apply social skills and how parents of children with autism can use these strategies to help their child become socially successful.

The Role of a BCBA

Board Certified Behavior Analysts (BCBAs) are certified professionals who specialize in the design, implementation and evaluation of behavior assessment and behavior-change interventions. They are highly trained in the field of Applied Behavior Analysis (ABA), a science-based field that has been proven to be effective in helping individuals with autism and other developmental disabilities gain meaningful social skills. BCBAs work with autistic individuals to assess their environment and behavior, identify potential areas for improvement, and develop and implement personalized intervention plans that are tailored to their needs.

BCBAs have expertise in a variety of areas, including understanding and teaching the generalization of social skills. Generalization is the process of learning a skill in one situation and then being able to apply the same skill in other situations. By teaching an individual how to generalize their social skills, BCBAs can help that individual become more successful in forming social relationships with their peers.

BCBAs can also help parents of children with autism by teaching them how to help their child generalize and apply social skills across different social environments. Parents are often the most important source of support for a child with autism, and teaching them how to help their child generalize and apply social skills can be invaluable. In addition, BCBAs can help parents understand the importance of creating natural learning opportunities in the home to help their child practice and gain mastery of the skills they are learning.

10 Tips on How an Autistic Person Can Teach Themselves to Generalize Social Skills

1. Have a structured and consistent routine. Establishing a consistent daily routine can help individuals with autism learn how to predict and anticipate what is coming next, helping them to feel more secure and make better social connections.

2. Practice social skills in different settings. Autistic individuals can benefit from practicing social skills in different settings, such as at home, at school, and in the community. This helps them to learn how to generalize the skills they have learned in one situation to other situations.

3. Ask for help and feedback. Don't hesitate to ask for help and feedback from family, friends, and professionals when needed. Receiving feedback can help autistic individuals understand how to apply social skills in different social settings.

4. Utilize visual supports. Visual supports, such as social stories and visual schedules, can be helpful in teaching social skills. Visual supports can provide autistic individuals with a way to remember and understand the expectations in different social situations.

5. Model appropriate social behavior. It is important for autistic individuals to observe and learn from the behavior of

others. By observing non-autistic individuals engaging in appropriate social behavior, autistic individuals can learn how to generalize and apply the same skills in different situations.

6. Practice role-playing. Role-playing can be a helpful tool in teaching social skills. By role-playing different social situations, autistic individuals can learn how to identify the appropriate behaviors in different situations.

7. Use reinforcement. Reinforcement is an important tool in teaching social skills. By providing positive reinforcement for appropriate behavior, autistic individuals can learn to generalize the skills they have learned in one situation to other situations.

8. Be patient. Learning to generalize and apply social skills in different social environments can take time. It is important to be patient and to understand that learning how to effectively communicate and interact with others is a process.

9. Set achievable goals. Setting achievable goals is a key component of learning how to generalize and apply social skills. It is important to set goals that are realistic and achievable, and to celebrate successes along the way.

10. Seek out professional help. If needed, seek out the help of a qualified professional who specializes in teaching social skills to individuals with autism. A

qualified professional, such as a BCBA, can provide valuable guidance and support on helping an individual with autism generalize and apply social skills in different social environments.

5 Tips for Parents of Children With Autism

1. Create a supportive environment. It is important to create a supportive and nurturing environment at home to help your child with autism learn how to interact and communicate with others.

2. Use visual supports. Utilize visual supports, such as social stories and visual schedules, to help your child understand and remember the expectations of different social situations.

3. Model appropriate social behavior. Model appropriate social behavior for your child. This can help your child understand how to act in different social settings.

4. Provide positive reinforcement. Provide positive reinforcement for appropriate behavior to help your child learn how to generalize and apply social skills.

5. Seek out professional help. If needed, seek out the help of a qualified professional, such as a BCBA, to provide guidance and support on helping your child generalize and apply social skills.

Conclusion

In conclusion, a BCBA can play a vital role in helping autistic individuals learn how to generalize and apply social skills across different social environments. By teaching individuals how to generalize their social skills and teaching parents how to help their child generalize and apply social skills, BCBAs can help autistic individuals become more successful in forming meaningful relationships with others. This essay has provided ten tips on how an autistic individual can teach themselves how to generalize and apply social skills across different social environments, as well as five tips for parents of children with autism on how to help their child become socially successful. With the support of a qualified professional, such as a BCBA, individuals with autism can learn the important skills of generalizing and applying social skills and become successful in forming meaningful relationships with others.

6 DAILY ADAPTIVE LIVING SKILLS VS SOCIAL SKILLS

Introduction

Autism is a complex disorder that affects an individual's social and communication skills, and can make everyday tasks such as daily adaptive living skills and social skills more challenging. Applied Behavior Analysis (ABA) is an evidence-based approach that has been used to teach individuals with autism to successfully participate in daily adaptive living skills and social skills. ABA is not a "one size fits all" approach, but can be tailored to the individual's specific abilities and needs. It is important to assess the individual's current level of functioning and create individualized teaching plans that are tailored to their abilities and goals. Furthermore, it is important to not use functioning labels with autism and instead use functioning levels. This allows for growth and development of skills over time as the individual learns and grows.

In this essay, we will compare and contrast daily adaptive living skills and social skills with autism and ABA. We will discuss how daily adaptive living skills work on lower-level skillsets, while social skills are higher-level skills. We will discuss the importance of not using functioning labels with autism and instead using functioning levels. We will discuss how it is important to meet the learner where they are at in their functioning level. We will discuss how for some learners daily adaptive living skills have social validity, and for other learners, social skills have more social validity. We will also provide 10 examples of daily adaptive living skills and 10 examples of social skills.

Daily Adaptive Living Skills

Daily adaptive living skills refer to everyday tasks that an individual needs to be able to complete in order to live independently. These skills include basic self-care, appropriate hygiene, and completing tasks such as cleaning and grocery shopping. Daily adaptive living skills are usually lower-level skillsets that an individual learns in order to be able to participate in daily life. ABA can be used to teach these skills to people with autism. For example, ABA can be used to teach an individual how to brush their teeth, complete a grocery list, or use public transportation.

ABA can also be used to teach higher-level skills such as life planning, budgeting, and job readiness skills. These skills can be important for an individual with autism to be successful in the workplace or in their daily life. ABA can also be used to teach problem-solving skills, which can help an individual with autism to identify their own strategies for dealing with challenging situations.

Social Skills

Social skills refer to the ability to interact with other people. Social skills involve being able to understand and interpret social cues, maintain appropriate eye contact, and communicate effectively. Social skills are usually higher-level skillsets that take more practice and repetition to learn and master. ABA can be used to teach social skills to individuals with autism. For example, ABA can be used to teach an individual how to initiate and maintain conversations, identify facial expressions and body language, and manage emotions in social situations.

ABA can also be used to teach self-advocacy skills, which involve being able to identify and express needs in a socially appropriate manner. Self-advocacy skills are important for individuals with autism to be able to navigate social situations and advocate for themselves.

Functioning Labels vs. Functioning Levels

It is important to not use functioning labels, such as "high functioning" or "low functioning", with autism and instead use functioning levels. Functioning labels are not accurate descriptors of an individual's abilities or potential. They can also be damaging to an individual's self-esteem and can limit their potential. It is important to meet the individual where they are at in their functioning level and provide individualized instruction to meet their needs and goals.

For some individuals, daily adaptive living skills may have more social validity than social skills. This means that the individual may find it easier or more acceptable to use daily adaptive living skills in social situations. For other learners, social skills may have more social validity. This means that the individual may find it easier or more acceptable to use social skills in social situations.

Conclusion

In conclusion, daily adaptive living skills and social skills are important skills for individuals with autism to learn in order to be successful in their daily life. ABA can be used to teach these skills to individuals with autism. It is important to assess the individual's functioning level and create individualized teaching plans that are tailored to their abilities and goals. It is also important to not use functioning labels and instead use functioning levels. This allows for growth and development of skills over time as the individual learns and grows. For some learners, daily adaptive living skills may have more social validity than social skills, while for other learners, social skills may have more social validity.

Examples of Daily Adaptive Living Skills:

• Grooming: brushing teeth, combing

hair, and taking a shower.

• Meal preparation: following recipes, grocery shopping, and meal planning.

• Household chores: doing laundry, cleaning, and organizing.

• Money management: budgeting and managing finances.

• Time management: setting goals and managing time efficiently.

• Self-care: recognizing personal needs and managing stress.

• Social Skills: initiating and maintaining conversations, recognizing facial expressions and body language, and managing emotions in social situations.

• Self-Advocacy: identifying and expressing needs in a socially appropriate manner.

• Vocational Skills: job readiness skills

and job seeking skills.

• Problem-Solving Skills: identifying strategies for dealing with challenging situations.

Examples of Social Skills:

• Greeting people: making eye contact and smiling.

• Conversation: using appropriate language, taking turns in conversations, and asking open-ended questions.

• Following Instructions: understanding and following directions.

• Building relationships: making friends and engaging in social activities.

• Handling emotions: recognizing and managing emotions in social situations.

• Negotiation: compromising and

problem-solving.

• Conflict resolution: managing
disagreements in a respectful manner.

• Listening: actively listening,
understanding, and responding to others.

• Self-regulation: managing emotions,
controlling behavior, and staying
focused.

• Sharing: taking turns and understanding
personal boundaries.

7. LOWER-LEVEL DAILY ADAPTIVE LIVING SKILLS

Introduction

Adaptive living skills are the skills that individuals need to successfully live and manage life's activities independently. These skills are essential for children and adults with autism and other developmental disorders, as they can help them to remain safe, interact with others, take care of themselves, and achieve autonomy. Adaptive living skills are skills such as cooking, dressing, brushing teeth, communication, problem-solving, money management, and many more. The importance of these skills lies in the fact that they are the doorway to independence, they provide people with the means to be successful and participate in our society.

Daily Adaptive Living Skills: What are They?

Daily adaptive living skills are the skills that individuals with autism and other developmental disorders need to perform daily activities and tasks. These skills include a wide range of activities, such as self-care skills, communication skills, problem-solving skills, and money management skills. They are the essential skills that are needed to perform everyday tasks, and they are often taken for granted by those who do not have a disability.

Daily adaptive living skills are important because they provide individuals with the means to be independent, to be self-sufficient, and to take part in society. They are the stepping stones to autonomy and success. They are also crucial for the development of higher-level social skills. Without the ability to perform daily adaptive living skills, people would be unable to learn higher-level social skills and would be unable to participate in society.

Examples of Daily Adaptive Living Skills

Daily adaptive living skills can be quite

different for those with level 3 autism compared to those with level 1 autism. Here are 10 examples of daily adaptive living skills for someone with level 3 autism:

1. Self-care skills such as brushing teeth, getting dressed, and washing one's hands.

2. Communication skills such as giving a simple greeting or responding to someone's question.

3. Toilet training skills.

4. Self-soothing techniques such as deep breathing and counting to 10.

5. Motor skills such as writing and cutting with scissors.

6. Social skills such as initiating conversations and maintaining eye

contact.

7. Money management skills such as counting change and making a purchase.

8. Problem-solving skills such as learning how to break a problem down into its component parts and finding a solution.

9. Time management skills such as staying on task and completing tasks on time.

10. Kitchen skills such as preparing a simple meal or snack.

Here are 10 examples of daily adaptive living skills for someone with level 1 autism:

1. Self-care skills such as brushing teeth, taking a shower or bath, and getting dressed.

2. Communication skills such as using facial expressions, gestures, and body language.

3. Toilet training skills.

4. Self-soothing techniques such as deep breathing and counting to 10.

5. Motor skills such as dressing oneself and cutting with scissors.

6. Social skills such as initiating conversations and maintaining eye contact.

7. Money management skills such as counting coins and making a purchase.

8. Problem-solving skills such as breaking a problem down into its component parts and finding a solution.

9. Time management skills such as staying on task and completing tasks on time.

10. Kitchen skills such as preparing a simple meal or snack.

Strategies for Teaching Adaptive Living Skills to Children with Autism

Teaching daily adaptive living skills to children with autism can be a difficult but rewarding task. It requires patience, understanding, and a committed approach. Here are 10 useful strategies that parents and professionals can use to teach these skills to children with autism:

1. Start by breaking down tasks into simple, achievable steps.

2. Use visual aids and pictorial cues to help children understand what is expected of them.

3. Use positive reinforcement to encourage the child to perform the task correctly.

4. Give the child plenty of time and space to learn the new skills.

5. Provide the child with plenty of practice and repetition to help them develop the skills.

6. Break tasks into small achievable chunks and provide frequent rewards for completing each one.

7. Model the desired behavior for the child and encourage them to imitate it.

8. Involve the child in the learning process by asking them questions and discussing their progress.

9. Provide clear and consistent feedback to help the child understand what they need to work on.

10. Stay calm and patient even when the child becomes frustrated or overwhelmed.

Motivating Your Autistic Child to Learn Adaptive Living Skills

Motivation is key to teaching daily adaptive living skills to children with autism. It is important to remember that children with autism often have difficulty with motivation and may need extra support and encouragement to stay on task and persist in the face of difficulty. Here are 10 strategies you can use to motivate your autistic child to learn adaptive living skills:

1. Set achievable goals and provide rewards for achieving them.

2. Allow the child to have input into the learning process, by letting them choose tasks they are interested in.

3. Break tasks into small, achievable steps and provide frequent rewards for completing each one.

4. Use a reward system such as a sticker chart or point system to motivate the child to stay on track.

5. Use visual aids and prompts to help the child stay focused on the task.

6. Use positive reinforcement and praise for correct responses and good behavior.

7. Provide a distraction-free environment to help the child stay on track.

8. Create fun and engaging activities to keep the child motivated.

9. Give the child plenty of time and space to complete tasks.

10. Give the child breaks when needed, to prevent them from becoming overwhelmed.

The Relationship Between Higher-Level Social Skills and Daily Adaptive Living Skills

While daily adaptive living skills are essential for individuals with autism and other developmental disorders, they are often not enough to allow them to participate fully in society. This is because daily adaptive living skills do not always include higher-level social skills, such as those needed to interact with peers, understand social cues, and maintain relationships. Without the ability to understand and use higher-level social skills, daily adaptive living skills can be useless in a social setting.

To be successful in life, it is essential for individuals with autism and other developmental disorders to learn higher-level social skills. These skills are essential for individuals to interact with others and make friends, to understand and respond appropriately to social cues, and to handle difficult social situations. It is important to remember that while daily adaptive living skills can help individuals to be safe and independent, these skills are often not enough to allow them to participate fully in society without the development of higher-level social skills.

Conclusion

Daily adaptive living skills are essential for individuals with autism and other developmental disorders, as they provide them with the skills needed to be independent, self-sufficient, and successful. They are also necessary for the development of higher-level social skills, which are essential for individuals to interact with others, understand social cues, and make friends. This is why it is important for parents and professionals to understand what daily adaptive living skills are and how to teach them to children with autism. Parents and professionals can use the strategies discussed in this chapter to help children with autism learn daily adaptive living skills, while also providing them with motivation and encouragement to stay on track. In conclusion, it is important to remember that daily adaptive living skills are essential but are often not enough to allow individuals to participate fully in society without the development of higher-level social skills.

8 HIGHER-LEVEL SOCIAL SKILLS

Social skills are an essential component of everyday living. They are the tool with which we interact with one another and form relationships with people we know, as well as those we don't. High-level social skills are the skills we use to effectively communicate, maintain relationships, and build trust. These are essential for success in life, as social skills are necessary for both personal and professional growth.

Daily Adaptive Living Skills (DALS) refers to the basic skills needed to perform everyday tasks such as housekeeping, hygiene, and money management. DALS are important because they serve as the foundation for higher level skills, such as social skills. Without these basic skills, it is difficult, if not impossible, to perform more advanced tasks. DALS are also the skills that often get taken for granted. We often expect someone to have the ability to do these tasks, so we don't think twice about them.

Social validity is a term used to describe the degree to which a person is accepted by their peers and/or society. People with disabilities, such as autism, can have a hard time obtaining social validity due to the challenges they face. Higher level social skills may have more social validity for someone with autism than someone without. This is because those with autism may face greater challenges in the social world and therefore the skills required to interact in this world may be more difficult for them to obtain.

For someone with lower levels of autism,

such as level 1, higher level social skills may be easier to obtain. They may have the ability to learn basic social skills such as eye contact, facial expressions, and conversational turn-taking. As a person progresses to higher levels, such as level 3, the skills required become more complex. These can include understanding sarcasm and humor, engaging in conversations about others, and being able to maintain relationships with peers.

Social validity builds with each skill we learn. For example, if we know how to identify coins then we would also want to know how to have small talk with the person giving us change. On the other hand, if we do not know how to use the daily adaptive living skill of identifying coins then creating small talk with the person giving us change may not be a socially valid skill to us. People are not attracted to us based on our daily adaptive living skills because these skills are taken for granted. Instead, people are attracted to how we make them feel. Therefore, it is important to be able to use social skills in order to make others feel comfortable and create meaningful connections.

Social skills coaching is an intervention that is used to help people with autism learn and practice more advanced, higher-level social skills. This can include role-playing, practice conversations, and learning how to interact in different social settings. Social skills coaches provide guidance and support to help someone better understand social cues and how to interact with others in a positive way.

Applied behavior analysis (ABA) is another intervention used to help teach social skills. This type of intervention is more structured than social skills coaching and is often used to teach more concrete skills such as following instructions and demonstrating appropriate behavior. This type of intervention is often used in combination with social skills coaching to address more complex social skills.

In conclusion, social skills are a vital part of everyday life and are necessary for both personal and professional development. They are also essential for obtaining social validity. Social skills are built on a foundation of daily adaptive living skills. Without these basic skills, it is difficult to perform more advanced tasks. Social skills coaches and applied behavior analysis (ABA) are two interventions used to help people with autism learn and practice higher-level social skills. They are important for helping to build social validity, as those with autism may face greater challenges when it comes to social interactions.

Social skills are the tools and behaviors we use to interact with the people around us. From the way we say hello to the way we react to other people's emotions, social skills are the key to meaningful and successful relationships. In order for us to truly understand the importance of social skills, it's important to understand why they are so important and how to use them effectively.

Social skills are important for everyone,

but they are especially important for people with autism. Many people with autism struggle to learn and understand social skills on their own, and they often need help and guidance to be able to master them. This essay will discuss the importance of social skills, the reasons they have social validity in relationships, and strategies that parents and professionals can use to help people with autism learn, practice, and generalize these skills.

The importance of social skills cannot be understated. Being able to interact with other people successfully, understand their emotions, and respond in the right way is essential for all of us. Social skills allow us to form meaningful relationships, navigate social situations, and communicate our thoughts and feelings. Furthermore, most of us use social skills unconsciously, without even thinking about it.

These skills are especially important for people with autism, since they often struggle to learn and master them on their own. It's important for parents and professionals to understand why social skills are so important, and to be aware of the reasons why they have social validity in relationships. It's also important to know the best strategies to use to help young learners with autism learn these skills.

Here are 10 reasons why social skills have social validity in relationships:

1. Social skills are the foundation of meaningful relationships. They allow us

to communicate our thoughts and feelings, understand the emotions of others, and form meaningful connections.

2. Social skills help us navigate social situations. By understanding the right way to interact with people, we can better understand and handle social situations.

3. Social skills help us understand our emotions. By understanding and responding appropriately to the emotions of others, we can learn to control and understand our own emotions.

4. Social skills allow us to express ourselves. By knowing how to say the right things in the right way, we can express ourselves more effectively and clearly.

5. Social skills can help us build confidence. When we know how to interact with people in the right way, it can help us build our confidence.

6. Social skills allow us to build self-esteem. When we know how to interact with people and understand their emotions, this can help us build our self-esteem.

7. Social skills help us form trust. By understanding people and responding appropriately to their emotions, we can build trust.

8. Social skills can help us build relationships. When we know how to

interact with people, it's easier to build and maintain relationships.

9. Social skills can help us handle challenges. By learning and practicing social skills, we can better handle social challenges.

10. Social skills can help us achieve our goals. By knowing how to interact with people in the right way, we can better achieve our goals.

Now that we've discussed why social skills are important and why they have social validity in relationships, let's talk about strategies that parents and professionals can use to help young learners with autism learn these skills.

One effective strategy is natural environment teaching. This involves teaching social skills in the contexts in which they are likely to be used. For example, if a child is having difficulty understanding how to greet someone, a parent or professional can model this behavior in a natural setting, such as at the grocery store or in the park. This way, the learner can practice the skill in a natural setting and understand how it works.

Another strategy is to use visual supports. Visual supports can be helpful for people with autism, since they often need extra help understanding and processing information. Visual supports can include pictures, charts, diagrams, and other visuals that can help the learner understand the social skill being taught.

Social stories are another useful strategy. Social stories are short stories that are designed to help the learner understand how to act in social situations. They can be used to explain the different steps involved in a social skill, as well as how to react in different situations.

Role-playing is another effective strategy. This involves creating a pretend situation in which the learner has to practice the social skill being taught. For example, the learner might role-play a conversation with a person they are meeting for the first time. This can be an effective way to help the learner practice the social skill in a safe and controlled environment.

Finally, reinforcement is an important strategy. Reinforcement involves rewarding the learner for their accomplishments, which can help encourage them to continue practicing and mastering the skill. This can be done in the form of verbal praise, tangible rewards, or a combination of both.

These are just a few of the strategies that parents and professionals can use to help young learners with autism learn social skills. Once the learner has mastered a social skill, it's important to help them generalize and apply that skill across different contexts and environments. Here are 3 strategies to help learners generalize and apply social skills:

1. Use coaching. Coaching involves providing the learner with guidance and

support as they practice and master the social skill. This can involve helping the learner practice the skill in different contexts, offering feedback, and providing positive reinforcement.

2. Provide opportunities for practice. It's important to give the learner as many opportunities as possible to practice the social skill. This can involve attending social gatherings, having conversations with family and friends, or participating in activities that require the use of the skill.

3. Model social skills. Modeling is another effective strategy for generalizing social skills. This involves demonstrating the right way to use the skill in different contexts. For example, if a learner is having difficulty understanding how to

greet someone, a parent or professional can model this behavior in a natural setting, such as at the grocery store or in the park.

Social skills are essential for everyone, but they are especially important for people with autism. Understanding why social skills have social validity in relationships, as well as strategies to help people with autism learn, practice, and apply these skills is essential for parents and professionals. By using the strategies discussed in this essay, parents and professionals can help young learners with autism learn and master social skills, and help them generalize and apply those skills in different contexts and environments.

9 CONTEXT IS KING

Context is King in Social Behavior and Applied Behavior Analysis

Context is an invaluable tool in social

behavior and Applied Behavior Analysis (ABA). Put simply, context is the circumstances that give a particular event meaning. It is essential to consider the context in which any behavior occurs in order to understand why it happened and what it means. Context is king in social behavior, as it provides the necessary clues to help explain why someone did something and what the meaning of their actions is.

In the context of ABA, context is even more important. ABA is the science of behavior and involves using evidence-based practices to help people change their behavior. It is essential to understand the context in which a behavior occurs in order to understand why it happened, what is likely to happen next, and most importantly, how to intervene and modify the behavior.

Context plays a major role in social behavior and ABA because it helps us to understand why someone is behaving in a particular manner and why that behavior makes sense in the context of the situation. This understanding can then be used to improve communication and social skills, which can in turn lead to improved outcomes.

In the case of autism, context is even more important because individuals with autism may not be able to understand the context of their behavior. This means that they may not be able to understand why they are behaving in a certain way and why it is wrong or inappropriate. In addition, individuals with autism may not be able to recognize the cues or signals that are used to communicate in social situations. Because of this, it is essential to understand the context in which a behavior occurs in order to help individuals with autism develop their social skills.

Context is also important in social behavior because it can help us to identify why someone is behaving in a particular way and how we can help them to change their behavior. For example, if someone is behaving in an aggressive manner, we can look at the context in which the behavior occurred to determine why the person may be behaving in this manner. We can then intervene and help the person to modify their behavior.

Context is also essential in ABA as it can help us to understand why a particular behavior is occurring, what it means, and how to intervene and modify it. For example, if someone is engaging in a self-injurious behavior, we can look at the context in which the behavior occurs in order to understand why it is happening, what it means, and how can help the person to move away from that behavior.

One of the most important examples of why context is king in social behavior and ABA is the story of a woman with autism who became pregnant as a result of a major contextual error. This woman had been taught by her parents that she could not get pregnant until she got married. However, having autism she interpreted this statement very literally, believing that she physically or scientifically could not become pregnant until she got married. As a result, she did not use protection and became pregnant.

This story is an excellent example of why context is so important in social behavior and ABA. This woman had misinterpreted the contextual cues of her parents' statement, resulting in her becoming pregnant. In addition, her parents' statement was also not in line with what was expected of her behaviorally, as it did not contain any information about how to protect herself from becoming pregnant. This story illustrates why it is so important to understand the context in which a behavior occurs in order to help individuals with autism to interpret contextual cues and understand how their behavior should be modified.

Another example of why context is king in social behavior and ABA is the concept of social step 1 through 787. This concept is based on the idea that an individual with autism is a "black and white" social thinker and will often skip from social step 1 to step 787. This means that they will not consider the context in which a behavior occurs or understand why it is appropriate or inappropriate in that context. For example, an individual with autism may not understand why it is not appropriate to swear in a library or why it is inappropriate to hug someone they have just met. By understanding the context in which a behavior occurs, we can help individuals with autism to understand why certain behaviors are appropriate or inappropriate in different contexts.

Finally, context is also important in social behavior and ABA because it can help us to develop better communication and social skills. Context is essential for effective communication, as it helps us to understand the meaning behind someone's words and actions. For example, if someone says "I love you", the context in which they said it (e.g. whether they were saying it in a romantic or platonic context) can tell us a lot about what they were trying to communicate. By understanding the context in which a behavior occurs, we can help individuals with autism to develop better social skills and effectively communicate with others.

In conclusion, context is an essential tool in social behavior and ABA. It provides us with the necessary clues to understand why someone is behaving in a certain manner and how we can help them to modify their behavior. It also helps us to develop better communication and social skills and to understand the context in which a behavior occurs in order to help individuals with autism to interpret contextual cues and modify their behavior. Context is king in social behavior and ABA and is essential for effective communication and the ability to understand and modify behavior.

10 THE GREEN DOT

When it comes to an autistic person's literal thinking and their relationship with social media, especially Facebook messenger, the green dot is one of the most important symbols to consider. For an autistic person, the green dot next to someone's name on Facebook messenger may appear to mean that the person is sitting there waiting to chat, even though this is rarely the case. In this essay, I will explain why the green dot on Facebook messenger can be confusing to an autistic person, the impact it can have on their mental health, and some strategies they can use to help manage the situation.

Autistic people tend to have a hard time

with figurative language and abstract concepts, which can make it difficult for them to interpret nonverbal cues. When they try to interpret the green dot on Facebook messenger, they may assume that the person is actively online and ready to engage in a chat. This isn't always the case, however, as the person may be away from the device, busy with something else, or simply not interested in replying to the message. Autistic people may also assume that the green dot still appears even when the user has left the page and is not actively engaged in a conversation, which isn't always true.

This confusion can lead to anxiety and frustration for an autistic person, particularly if they are reaching out to connect with someone and don't receive a response. Autistic people tend to interpret things literally and may not understand why someone isn't responding or that they are busy with other things. It can feel like the person isn't interested in talking with them or that they have been ignored. This can lead to feelings of rejection, loneliness, and depression.

In addition to this, the green dot can also cause confusion when it comes to navigating conversations. Autistic people may become fixated on the green dot and interpret it as a sign that the person is ready to chat, rather than considering the context of the conversation and waiting for a response. This can lead to a lot of back and forth messages, which can quickly become overwhelming and exhausting.

To help manage this confusion and anxiety, autistic people can use a few strategies. One strategy is to give the other person a reasonable amount of time to respond. This helps to avoid the feeling of being ignored and gives the other person an opportunity to reply. Autistic people can also try to use the "seen" feature when sending messages, as this can provide an indication of whether the other person has read the message or not. It can also be helpful to remember that the green dot does not always mean that the person is actively online and ready to chat, and to be patient when waiting for a response.

Finally, it is important for autistic people to be aware of their own emotions and to take a break if they are feeling overwhelmed or anxious. Taking a break can help to take the focus away from the green dot and the feeling of being ignored, and can provide time to regroup and think about the situation in a calmer state of mind.

Overall, it is important to remember that the green dot on Facebook messenger can be confusing and anxiety-inducing for an autistic person. That said, with the right strategies and awareness of their own emotions, autistic people can manage these feelings and use social media to connect with others in a more positive way.

Nature Vs. Nurture: The Tale of Discrete Trial Training and Natural Environment Teaching

11 HOW TO USE SOCIAL NETWORKING SITES SAFELY

Introduction

In the digital age, social media platforms such as Facebook and Instagram are widely used by people of all ages. As a result, it is important that parents and professionals take the time to ensure that their children are using these platforms in an appropriate manner. By providing children with the necessary guidance and support, they can learn to use Facebook and Instagram appropriately. In this essay, 25 tips and strategies will be outlined that can help parents and professionals teach children of all ages how to use Facebook and Instagram in a safe and responsible way.

1. Be aware of the age requirements for the platforms

Facebook and Instagram have established age requirements for their respective platforms. According to their terms of service, users must be at least 13 years old to use Facebook and 13 years old to use Instagram. It is important for parents and professionals to be aware of these age requirements and ensure that children are of appropriate age before signing up for either of these platforms.

2. Teach children how to recognize scams and suspicious content

Facebook and Instagram are popular targets for scams and other malicious content. Parents and professionals should ensure that their children are familiar with the signs of suspicious content, such as links that lead to unknown websites or requests for personal information.

3. Establish rules for online behavior

Before allowing children to use Facebook and Instagram, parents and professionals should establish clear rules for online behavior. These rules should include an agreed-upon amount of time that can be spent online, as well as guidelines for acceptable behavior.

4. Monitor online activity

It is important for parents and professionals to monitor their children's online activity. This can be done through tools such as parental control apps and monitoring software. These tools can help ensure that children are using the platforms in an appropriate manner.

5. Discuss the importance of privacy

Parents and professionals should explain to their children the importance of privacy and why it is important to keep personal information private. This includes information such as phone numbers, addresses, and financial information.

6. Teach children how to identify cyberbullying

Cyberbullying is a serious problem on both Facebook and Instagram. Parents and professionals should teach their children how to recognize cyberbullying and what to do if they are being targeted.

7. Explain the consequences of inappropriate behavior

Parents and professionals should explain to their children the potential consequences of inappropriate online behavior. This could include being banned from the platform or even legal action if the person is a minor.

8. Set up parental accounts

If possible, parents and professionals

should set up their own accounts on Facebook and Instagram. This will allow them to monitor their children's activity and help ensure that they are using the platforms appropriately.

9. Encourage open communication

Parents and professionals should encourage open communication between themselves and their children. This will help ensure that children feel comfortable coming to their parents or professionals with any questions or concerns they may have about using the platforms.

10. Discuss the potential risks of using the platforms

Parents and professionals should discuss with their children the potential risks of using the platforms, such as identity theft or cyberbullying. This will help ensure that children understand the importance of using the platforms safely and responsibly.

11. Engage in conversations about the platforms

Parents and professionals should engage in conversations with their children about the platforms. This could include discussing the latest features or discussing why they think certain features are inappropriate.

12. Encourage the use of privacy settings

Facebook and Instagram both have a variety of privacy settings that users can adjust to help keep their information private. Parents and professionals should encourage their children to use these settings to help protect their information and prevent unwanted posts or messages.

13. Remind children about the importance of "liking" responsibly

Parents and professionals should remind their children about the importance of "liking" responsibly. This includes refraining from "liking" inappropriate content or posts from strangers.

14. Explain the implications of sharing

personal information

Parents and professionals should explain to their children the implications of sharing personal information, such as phone numbers or addresses. They should explain that personal information can be used to target them in malicious ways and should only be shared with trusted friends or family.

15. Discuss the importance of reporting posts or messages

Parents and professionals should discuss with their children the importance of reporting posts or messages that they find inappropriate or offensive. This will help ensure that other users are not victimized by malicious content.

16. Explain the risks of oversharing

Parents and professionals should explain to their children the risks of oversharing. This includes posting too much personal information, such as a home address or phone number. It also includes posting content that could be deemed inappropriate, such as explicit photos or videos.

17. Encourage the use of strong passwords

Parents and professionals should encourage their children to use strong passwords for their accounts. Strong passwords should include a combination of numbers, symbols, and upper and lower case letters.

18. Explain the importance of not befriending strangers

Parents and professionals should explain to their children the importance of not befriending strangers on social media. This will help ensure that their information is not shared with people who may have malicious intentions.

19. Explain the consequences of sharing inappropriate content

Parents and professionals should explain to their children the potential consequences of sharing inappropriate content. This could include being banned from the platform or even legal action if the content is deemed to be illegal.

20. Explain the risks of "liking" posts from strangers

Parents and professionals should explain to their children the risks of "liking" posts from strangers. This could lead to the sharing of personal information with people who may have malicious intentions.

21. Explain the implications of "following" suspicious accounts

Parents and professionals should explain to their children the implications of "following" suspicious accounts. This could lead to the sharing of personal information with people who may have malicious intentions.

22. Discuss the potential consequences of inappropriate posts or messages

Parents and professionals should discuss with their children the potential consequences of inappropriate posts or messages. This could include being banned from the platform or even legal action if the content is deemed to be illegal.

23. Explain the dangers of linking accounts

Parents and professionals should explain to their children the dangers of linking accounts, such as Facebook and Instagram. This could lead to accounts being hacked or personal information being shared with strangers.

24. Explain the implications of "tagging" in photos or posts

Parents and professionals should explain to their children the implications of "tagging" in photos or posts. This could lead to personal information being shared with strangers or people with malicious intentions.

25. Explain the importance of being a good digital citizen

Finally, parents and professionals should explain to their children the importance of being a good digital citizen. This includes being aware of the potential risks of using the platforms and understanding the implications of their actions.

Conclusion

In conclusion, it is important for parents and professionals to take the necessary steps to ensure that their children are using Facebook and Instagram in an appropriate manner. By implementing the tips and strategies outlined in this essay, it is possible to ensure that children are using the platforms safely and responsibly.

Nature Vs. Nurture: The Tale of Discrete Trial Training and Natural Environment Teaching

12 GENERALIZATION AND APPLICATION OF A SOCIAL SKILL

Introduction

Social skills are the actions and behaviors used to interact with other people in society. These skills are vitally important in all areas of life, as they are necessary for successful communication and relationship building. Social skills also impact a person's ability to succeed in school, work, and personal relationships. Unfortunately, many people with autism spectrum disorder (ASD) may have difficulty acquiring, generalizing, and applying social skills in different contexts.

Generalizing and applying social skills

refers to the ability to use those skills in different social contexts. It is a critical skill for those on the autism spectrum, as it allows them to interact with people in a variety of settings and better understand social cues. Without the ability to generalize and apply social skills, individuals may find themselves struggling to fit in and connect with others, leading to social isolation and difficulty in many areas of life.

For those on the autism spectrum, learning technical social skills is the first step in generalizing and applying them in different social contexts. This involves the use of strategies to recognize and respond to the subtleties of the social world, such as body language, facial expressions, and tone of voice. Once these skills are mastered, individuals can then begin to apply them to different contexts.

The ability to generalize and apply social skills is vitally important for those on the autism spectrum, so it is important to understand how to help them do so. In this essay, the importance of learning technical social skills before generalizing and applying them in different contexts will be discussed, as well as 20 strategies that can be used to help an autistic person generalize and apply social skills in different social contexts.

The Importance of Learning Technical Social Skills

Technical social skills refer to the skills and strategies necessary to understand and interpret social cues, as well as respond appropriately in a variety of social contexts. This includes understanding body language, facial expressions, and tone of voice, as well as the use of appropriate language and conversation skills.

These technical social skills are essential for those on the autism spectrum, as they provide the foundation for understanding and responding appropriately to the subtleties of the social world. Without this knowledge, individuals may find themselves struggling to understand social cues, or may respond in ways that are seen as inappropriate or socially unacceptable.

Mastering technical social skills is the first step in helping an autistic person generalize and apply their skills in different contexts. It is important to note that while some individuals may be able to learn technical social skills quickly, others may need more time and practice. Therefore, providing ample opportunity to practice these skills is essential.

Once individuals have mastered technical social skills, they can then begin to apply them in different contexts. This is vitally important for those on the autism spectrum, as it allows them to interact with people in a variety of settings and better understand social cues. Without the ability to generalize and apply social skills, individuals may find themselves struggling to fit in and connect with others, leading to social isolation and difficulty in many areas of life.

Strategies for Generalizing and Applying

Social Skills in Different Contexts

Once an individual has learned technical social skills, the next step is to help them generalize and apply them in different contexts. This can be a difficult process, but there are several strategies that can be used to help an autistic person successfully generalize and apply their social skills. The following are 20 strategies that can be used to help an autistic person generalize and apply social skills in different social contexts.

1. Modeling: Modeling is a strategy in which the individual watches another person demonstrate a particular skill or behavior. This can be a helpful tool for those on the autism spectrum, as it allows them to observe the behavior and copy it in their own lives.

2. Repetition: Repetition is a powerful tool when it comes to helping an autistic person master a particular skill or behavior. By repeating the skill or behavior multiple times, the individual can become more familiar and comfortable with it and eventually be able to apply it in different contexts.

3. Role Playing: Role playing is a strategy in which the individual is put in a simulated situation and asked to practice a particular skill or behavior. This can be an effective tool for those on the autism spectrum, as it allows them to practice a skill or behavior in a low-stakes environment, thus increasing the likelihood of success when the skill or behavior is applied in a real-world context.

4. Social Stories: Social stories are a tool used to teach social skills to those on the autism spectrum. These stories provide a visual representation of a particular skill or behavior and can be used to help individuals better understand and apply it in different contexts.

5. Visual Aids: Visual aids, such as pictures, diagrams, and videos, can be used to help autistic individuals better understand and apply a particular skill or behavior. These aids can be used in combination with other strategies, such as modeling and role playing, to help the individual master the skill or behavior.

6. Social Scripts: Social scripts are a tool used to teach social skills to those on the

autism spectrum. These scripts provide a written representation of a particular skill or behavior and can be used to help individuals better understand and apply it in different contexts.

7. Video Modeling: Video modeling is a strategy in which the individual watches another person demonstrate a particular skill or behavior on a video. This can be an effective tool for those on the autism spectrum, as it allows them to observe the behavior and copy it in their own lives.

8. Social Media: Social media can be a powerful tool for those on the autism spectrum, as it allows them to interact with others in a safe, low-stakes environment. Through social media, individuals can practice and build upon their social skills in a variety of contexts.

9. Real-world Practice: Real-world practice is a valuable tool for those on the autism spectrum, as it allows them to apply their skills and behavior in real-life situations. This can be especially beneficial for those who may be struggling to generalize and apply their skills in different contexts.

10. Adaptive Technology: Adaptive technology can be a great tool for those on the autism spectrum, as it allows them to interact with others and practice their skills without the fear of repercussions. This can be a valuable tool for those who may be struggling to generalize and apply their skills in different contexts.

11. Practice in a Variety of Settings:

Practicing social skills in a variety of settings can be a helpful tool for those on the autism spectrum, as it allows them to become more comfortable and confident in their skills in different environments.

12. Trial and Error: Trial and error is a powerful tool for those on the autism spectrum, as it allows them to practice their skills and learn from their mistakes in a low-stakes environment.

13. Positive Reinforcement: Positive reinforcement is a strategy in which the individual is rewarded for performing a particular skill or behavior. This can be a helpful tool for those on the autism spectrum, as it provides motivation and encourages them to continue practicing and applying their skills in different contexts.

14. Visual Schedules: Visual schedules are a tool used to teach social skills to those on the autism spectrum. These schedules provide a visual representation of a particular skill or behavior and can be used to help individuals better understand and apply it in different contexts.

15. Social Groups: Social groups are a valuable tool for those on the autism spectrum, as they provide a safe, low-stakes environment in which individuals can practice and build upon their social skills.

16. Peer Support: Peer support is a valuable tool for those on the autism spectrum, as it allows them to interact

with others who are in similar situations and practice their skills in a safe and supportive environment.

17. Cognitive Behavioral Therapy: Cognitive behavioral therapy is a powerful tool for those on the autism spectrum, as it allows them to identify and address the thoughts and behaviors that are preventing them from succeeding. This can be a valuable tool for those who may be struggling to generalize and apply their skills in different contexts.

18. Visual Cues: Visual cues are a tool used to teach social skills to those on the autism spectrum. These cues provide a visual representation of a particular skill or behavior and can be used to help individuals better understand and apply it

in different contexts.

19. Systematic Instruction: Systematic instruction is a strategy in which the individual is taught a particular skill or behavior in a step-by-step manner. This can be an effective tool for those on the autism spectrum, as it allows them to take their time and better understand the skill or behavior before attempting to apply it in different contexts.

20. Social Skills Training Groups: Social skills training groups are an invaluable tool for those on the autism spectrum, as they provide an opportunity for individuals to practice their skills and receive feedback in a safe and supportive environment.

Conclusion

Social skills are vitally important for those on the autism spectrum, as they allow them to interact with others and better understand social cues. Unfortunately, many individuals may struggle to acquire, generalize, and apply these skills in different contexts. It is important to understand the importance of learning technical social skills before generalizing and applying them in different contexts.

The strategies discussed in this essay provide several tools for helping an autistic person generalize and apply social skills in different social contexts. These strategies can be used in combination with one another to create an effective and comprehensive plan for

helping an individual master and apply
their social skills.

Overall, it is vitally important for those
on the autism spectrum to learn,
generalize, and apply social skills in
different contexts. By understanding the
importance of technical social skills, as
well as providing strategies to help an
individual successfully generalize and
apply them in different contexts, we can
help those on the autism spectrum lead
successful and fulfilling lives.

13 48 KEY STRATEGIES BCBA'S CAN USE TO TEACH SOCIAL SKILLS TO AUTISTIC CHILDREN AND ADULTS

Introduction

Autism is a complex developmental disorder that affects a person's ability to communicate and interact with others. It is a spectrum disorder, meaning that its severity can vary greatly from person to person. People with autism may have difficulty in understanding and expressing emotions, interpreting social cues, and engaging in typical social interactions. It is estimated that 1 in 54 children in the United States is on the autism spectrum.

Individuals with autism may require more assistance to learn and develop social skills than their non-autistic peers. Individuals with autism may not always be aware of their own behaviors and may not understand the behavior of others, making it difficult for them to learn social skills on their own. Fortunately, Board Certified Behavior Analysts (BCBAs) can use evidence-based strategies to teach social skills to individuals with autism.

In this essay, we will examine 50 key strategies that BCBAs can use to help individuals with autism learn social skills. We will also discuss how BCBAs can help individuals with autism generalize and apply these skills to different social contexts and environments.

48 Key Strategies for Teaching Social Skills to Individuals with Autism

1. Modeling: Modeling is a common

strategy used by BCBAs to teach social skills to individuals with autism. The BCBA can model appropriate behaviors and interactions by demonstrating the desired behavior in a direct, instructional way. This strategy helps individuals with autism observe and learn the behavior by imitation.

2. Social Stories: Social stories are brief narratives that explain the appropriate behavior in a given social situation. BCBAs can use social stories to teach individuals with autism the appropriate behaviors to use in a variety of social contexts.

3. Role-Playing: Role-playing can be used to teach social skills to individuals with autism. By role-playing certain social situations, individuals with autism

can get practice in performing the desired behaviors.

4. Video Modeling: Video modeling is a form of modeling that is used to teach social skills to individuals with autism. The BCBA can use videos to demonstrate the desired behavior, which can help the individual better understand and remember the behavior.

5. Visual Supports: Visual supports such as pictures, diagrams, and charts can be used to help individuals with autism better understand the desired behaviors. These visual supports can help individuals with autism better comprehend the social skills being taught.

6. Social Scripts: Social scripts are a type of verbal instruction that can be used to teach social skills to individuals with autism. By providing specific instructions and describing the desired behavior in detail, BCBAs can help individuals with autism learn the appropriate social skills.

7. Self-Monitoring: Self-monitoring is a strategy wherein the individual with autism is taught to recognize and monitor their own behavior. This can help them better understand the social context and respond appropriately.

8. Systematic Instruction: Systematic instruction is a method of teaching social skills to individuals with autism in an organized, sequential way. By breaking down the desired behavior into smaller components, BCBAs can help individuals

with autism learn the behavior more effectively.

9. Positive Reinforcement: Positive reinforcement is a common strategy used by BCBAs to teach social skills to individuals with autism. By rewarding appropriate behaviors, BCBAs can help individuals with autism associate positive outcomes with the desired behaviors.

10. Social Skills Groups: Social skills groups are a form of group instruction that can help individuals with autism learn social skills. By being in a group setting, individuals with autism can observe and practice the desired behaviors in a natural environment.

11. Reward Systems: Reward systems

can be used to encourage individuals with autism to engage in the desired behaviors. By providing rewards for appropriate behavior, BCBAs can help individuals with autism better understand and remember the desired behaviors.

12. Response Cost: Response cost is a type of punishment strategy that can be used to reduce inappropriate behaviors. By using response cost, BCBAs can help individuals with autism better understand the consequences of their behavior.

13. Verbal Cues: Verbal cues are a form of verbal instruction that can be used to teach social skills to individuals with autism. By providing specific instructions, BCBAs can help individuals with autism better understand and remember the desired behaviors.

14. Structured Activities: Structured activities can be used to help individuals with autism practice the desired behaviors in a controlled environment. By providing structure, BCBAs can help individuals with autism practice the desired skills more effectively.

15. Problem-Solving: Problem-solving is a strategy that can be used to help individuals with autism understand and respond to social cues appropriately. BCBAs can help individuals with autism develop problem-solving skills by providing them with opportunities to practice the desired behaviors.

16. Visual Schedules: Visual schedules are a type of visual support that can be

used to help individuals with autism understand the expectations in a given social context. By providing a visual schedule, BCBAs can help individuals with autism anticipate and plan for the desired behaviors.

17. Self-Regulation Strategies: Self-regulation strategies can be used to help individuals with autism identify and manage their emotions in a given social context. BCBAs can help individuals with autism learn self-regulation strategies by modeling the behavior and providing verbal instruction.

18. Social Language Therapy: Social language therapy is a type of intervention that can be used to help individuals with autism better understand and use social language. BCBAs can help individuals

with autism learn the appropriate social language by providing instruction and modeling the desired behavior.

19. Peer-Mediated Intervention: Peer-mediated intervention is a strategy that can be used to help individuals with autism learn and practice social skills with their peers. BCBAs can help individuals with autism develop peer relationships by facilitating structured activities and providing verbal instruction.

20. Applied Behavior Analysis: Applied behavior analysis (ABA) is a form of intervention that is commonly used to teach social skills to individuals with autism. BCBAs can use ABA to assess behavior, develop intervention plans, and modify behaviors.

21. Self-Advocacy Training: Self-advocacy training is a type of intervention that can be used to help individuals with autism develop the skills they need to advocate for themselves in a social context. BCBAs can help individuals with autism learn self-advocacy skills by providing instruction and modeling the desired behavior.

22. Social Narratives: Social narratives are a type of intervention that can be used to help individuals with autism better understand the expectations in a given social context. BCBAs can help individuals with autism learn the appropriate social language by providing instruction and modeling the desired behavior.

23. Structured Practical Life Skills
Training: Structured practical life skills
training is a type of intervention that can
be used to help individuals with autism
develop the skills they need to function
independently in a social context. BCBAs
can help individuals with autism learn the
appropriate life skills by providing
instruction and modeling the desired
behavior.

24. Social Goals and Objectives Training:
Social goals and objectives training is a
type of intervention that can be used to
help individuals with autism develop the
skills they need to interact appropriately
with others. BCBAs can help individuals
with autism learn appropriate social
behaviors by establishing goals and
providing instruction and modeling.

25. Visual Prompts: Visual prompts are a type of visual support that can be used to help individuals with autism better understand the expectations in a given social context. By providing a visual prompt, BCBAs can help individuals with autism better comprehend the desired behavior.

26. Functional Behavioral Assessments: Functional behavioral assessments are a form of assessment that can be used to identify the function of a behavior. By conducting a functional behavioral assessment, BCBAs can better understand the individual's behavior and develop an appropriate intervention plan.

27. Task Analysis: Task analysis is a technique that can be used to break down a task into smaller, more manageable

steps. By breaking down the task into smaller steps, BCBAs can help individuals with autism better understand the desired behavior and learn it more effectively.

28. Cue-Based Instruction: Cue-based instruction is a form of instruction that can be used to teach social skills to individuals with autism. By providing cues, BCBAs can help individuals with autism better understand the desired behavior and remember it more effectively.

29. Cognitive Behavioral Therapy: Cognitive behavioral therapy (CBT) is a form of intervention that can be used to help individuals with autism learn how to regulate their emotions in a social context. BCBAs can help individuals

with autism learn the appropriate coping strategies and identify and manage their emotions more effectively.

30. Discrete Trial Training: Discrete trial training is a type of intervention that can be used to teach social skills to individuals with autism. By providing instruction and modeling the desired behavior, BCBAs can help individuals with autism learn the appropriate behavior more effectively.

31. Structured Play: Structured play is a type of intervention that can be used to help individuals with autism practice the desired behaviors in a natural environment. By providing structure, BCBAs can help individuals with autism practice the desired skills more effectively.

32. Social Problem-Solving Training:
Social problem-solving training is a type
of intervention that can be used to help
individuals with autism identify and
solve social problems. By providing
instruction and modeling the desired
behavior, BCBAs can help individuals
with autism develop the problem-solving
skills they need to interact appropriately
in a social context.

33. Instructional Technology:
Instructional technology can be used to
help individuals with autism learn social
skills. By using computers, tablets, and
other technologies, BCBAs can help
individuals with autism learn the desired
behaviors in a more engaging way.

34. Social Skill Games: Social skill games are a type of intervention that can be used to help individuals with autism practice the desired behaviors in a fun and engaging way. By using games, BCBAs can help individuals with autism learn the appropriate behavior more effectively.

35. Systematic Desensitization: Systematic desensitization is a form of intervention that can be used to help individuals with autism better manage their anxiety in a social context. By providing instruction and modeling the desired behavior, BCBAs can help individuals with autism learn relaxation strategies and develop the skills they need to interact appropriately in a social context.

36. Naturalistic Teaching Strategies:
Naturalistic teaching strategies are a type
of intervention that can be used to help
individuals with autism learn the desired
behaviors in a natural environment. By
providing instruction and modeling the
desired behavior, BCBAs can help
individuals with autism learn the
appropriate behavior more effectively.

37. Social Cognitive Theory: Social
cognitive theory is a form of intervention
that can be used to help individuals with
autism better understand the social
environment and learn the appropriate
behaviors. By providing instruction and
modeling the desired behavior, BCBAs
can help individuals with autism develop
the skills they need to interact
appropriately in a social context.

38. Picture Exchange Communication System: Picture exchange communication system (PECS) is a form of intervention that can be used to help individuals with autism learn the appropriate social language. By providing visual supports, BCBAs can help individuals with autism better understand the desired behavior and remember it more effectively.

39. Self-Management Training: Self-management training is a type of intervention that can be used to help individuals with autism learn how to manage their own behavior in a social context. By providing instruction and modeling the desired behavior, BCBAs can help individuals with autism develop the skills they need to interact appropriately in a social context.

40. Social Skills Assessments: Social skills assessments are a type of assessment that can be used to evaluate an individual's social skills. By conducting a social skills assessment, BCBAs can better understand the individual's social skills and develop an appropriate intervention plan.

41. Rehearsal and Fluency Training: Rehearsal and fluency training is a type of intervention that can be used to help individuals with autism learn the desired behaviors more effectively. By providing instruction and modeling the desired behavior, BCBAs can help individuals with autism practice and learn the behavior more quickly.

42. Functional Communication Training: Functional communication training is a form of intervention that can be used to help individuals with autism learn the appropriate social language. By providing instruction and modeling the desired behavior, BCBAs can help individuals with autism better understand and use the appropriate social language.

43. Videotape Self-Monitoring: Videotape self-monitoring is a type of intervention that can be used to help individuals with autism better understand their own behavior in a social context. By videotaping themselves, BCBAs can help individuals with autism observe and evaluate their own behavior and identify areas that need improvement.

44. Self-Awareness Training: Self-

awareness training is a type of intervention that can be used to help individuals with autism better understand their own behavior and the behaviors of others in a social context. By providing instruction and modeling the desired behavior, BCBAs can help individuals with autism develop the skills they need to interact appropriately in a social context.

45. Cognitive Restructuring: Cognitive restructuring is a type of intervention that can be used to help individuals with autism identify and challenge negative thoughts and beliefs in a social context. By providing instruction and modeling the desired behavior, BCBAs can help individuals with autism develop the skills they need to interact appropriately in a social context.

46. Relapse Prevention Training: Relapse prevention training is a type of intervention that can be used to help individuals with autism better manage their behaviors in a social context. By providing instruction and modeling the desired behavior, BCBAs can help individuals with autism identify triggers and develop strategies to prevent relapse.

47. Social Skill Instructional Strategies: Social skill instructional strategies are a type of intervention that can be used to help individuals with autism learn the desired behaviors. By providing instruction and modeling the desired behavior, BCBAs can help individuals with autism learn the appropriate behavior more effectively.

48. Systematic Exposure Training: Systematic exposure training is a type of intervention that can be used to help individuals with autism gradually increase their exposure to social situations. By providing instruction and modeling the desired behavior, BCBAs can help individuals with autism develop the skills they need to interact appropriately in a social context.

CONCLUSION

In conclusion, discrete trial training and
natural environment training are both
highly effective forms of applied
behavior analysis. Both approaches have
their own distinct advantages, and when
used in combination can produce
remarkable results.

Discrete trial training is a highly structured form of teaching in which a child is presented with a specific task and rewarded for correct responses. The advantages of this approach include the ability to quickly and precisely measure the success of a given task, the ability to rapidly modify tasks and responses, and the positive reinforcement of desired behaviors which can produce long-term results. Among the main disadvantages are the potential for a child to become overly dependent on rewards, and the fact that it may require more of a teacher's time to properly implement.

Natural environment teaching is an approach which emphasizes the use of natural context and objects to teach desired behaviors. The main advantages of this approach include the ability to increase a child's interest in the task, the ability to teach a variety of skills in a single session, and the ability to teach behaviors in a way that is more meaningful to the child. Among the main disadvantages are the difficulty of measuring success, the potential to be overwhelmed by the environment, and the difficulty of generalizing learned behaviors across contexts.

In the end, both approaches can be successful when used in combination. Discrete trial training can be used to quickly and precisely teach behaviors, while natural environment teaching can be used to provide meaning and context to learned behaviors. By understanding the advantages and disadvantages of each approach, educators can develop a well-rounded and effective plan for teaching desired behaviors.

ABOUT THE AUTHOR

Author, autism expert, and trombone player from Huntington, Indiana living in Fort Wayne. Exploring the world through travel and connecting with family - especially my two nieces and my sister. Passionate about social behavior.

www.travisebreeding.com

travis@travisebreeding.com

venmo is breete03

Nature Vs. Nurture: The Tale of Discrete Trial Training and Natural
Environment Teaching

157

Nature Vs. Nurture: The Tale of Discrete Trial Training and Natural Environment Teaching